GOD IS NOT ANGRY

Justice, Love, and the Character of God

By Benjamin Liles

Many believe the Bible portrays an angry, controlling God – but Scripture tells a different story. From Proverbs to the cross of Christ, the Bible reveals a God whose justice flows from compassion, patience, and love, not fear and domination. This book traces that consistent thread, showing that God is slow to anger, focused on restoration, and committed to drawing humanity back into His care. If Jesus truly lived and died on the cross, the vision of God is not only coherent—it is trustworthy.

Copyright © 2026 Benjamin Liles

All rights reserved.

No part of this book may be reproduced or transmitted in any form or by any means, electronic or mechanical, including photocopying, recording, or by any information storage and retrieval system, without permission in writing from the publisher.

ISBN: 9798246761434

Printed in the United States of America

DEDICATION

For all those before me: those who truly knew and fought to stay in the arms and the grace of Jesus Christ, our Lord and Savior

CONTENTS

Contents

CONTENTS

The Modern Accusation: "The Bible Is Outdated and Harmful"

Human Nature vs. Divine Justice

"Slow to Anger": The Most Repeated Description of God

Justice as Restoration, Not Retribution

The Beatitudes: Justice Turned Upside Down

"How Often I Wanted to Gather You": Love Without Coercion

Love Is Not Easily Angered: Paul and the Shape of Divine Love

The Cross: Where Justice and Love Meet

Resurrection: God's Verdict on Humanity

Faith Without Fear: Living Under Restorative Justice

Living Restored:? Justice, Mercy, and Human Continuity

God Is For You

What You Thought Was Against You Was Guarding You

The Modern Accusation: "The Bible Is Outdated and Harmful"

In the modern world, few ideas are met with more suspicion than the claim that the Bible is a trustworthy guide to truth, justice, or human flourishing. For many, Scripture is no longer viewed as sacred wisdom but as a relic of a more primitive age—an artifact shaped by power, fear, and social control rather than truth. The God of the Bible, critics argue, is not loving but volatile; not just but authoritarian; not merciful but cruel.

This accusation is not shouted only from the margins. It is spoken quietly in classrooms, online forums, podcasts, and dinner-table conversations. It is voiced by skeptics, former believers, theologians, and people who once loved the church but left wounded and disillusioned. Increasingly, the critique is not simply *"I don't believe in God,"* but rather *"I reject the God the Bible seems to describe."*

According to this view, Scripture was written primarily to **subjugate people**—to legitimize hierarchy, suppress dissent, and enforce obedience by invoking divine authority. God becomes a tool of control, and justice becomes a weapon wielded by the powerful. In this framework, obedience is demanded, fear is cultivated, and punishment is framed as righteousness.

If this accusation is accurate, then the Bible is not merely mistaken—it is dangerous.

And yet, before the Bible can be dismissed, something far more uncomfortable must be addressed.

The Assumptions Beneath the Accusation

Most modern critiques of the Bible rest on two deeply held assumptions.

The first is that **divine authority necessarily undermines human freedom**. If God commands, then humans must submit. If Scripture claims moral authority, then individual conscience must be silenced. In this view, faith and freedom are opposites, and obedience is inherently oppressive.

The second assumption is that **biblical justice equals cruelty**. Judgment is interpreted as rage, holiness as intolerance, and moral boundaries as evidence of hostility toward human autonomy. God's anger is seen as emotional volatility rather than moral restraint, and punishment is assumed to be His primary concern.

Together, these assumptions create a picture of God that is not merely unappealing, but morally suspect. A God who rules through fear cannot be trusted. A God who delights in punishment cannot be good. A God who demands obedience without compassion cannot be worthy of worship.

Many people do not reject God because they want to rebel. They reject God because they believe **they must**—because the God they have been shown appears incompatible with love, justice, or human dignity.

But here is the critical problem:

If this picture of God is accurate, then **Christianity collapses under its own weight**.

The Cross as the Test Case

Christian faith does not hinge on abstract ideas, philosophical systems, or moral platitudes. It hinges on a historical claim: that Jesus of Nazareth lived, taught, was crucified under Roman authority, and that His death holds redemptive meaning.

The cross is not a footnote in Christianity. It is the center.

The Gospel of John expresses this without ambiguity:

"For God so loved the world, that he gave his one and only Son, that whoever believes in him should not perish, but have eternal life. For God didn't send his Son into the world to judge the world, but that the world should be saved through him."
— **Gospel of John 3:16–17 (WEB)**

If God's fundamental posture toward humanity is domination or cruelty, this passage becomes incoherent. Tyrants do not sacrifice themselves for their subjects. Manipulators do not absorb injustice at their own expense. Authoritarians do not offer salvation instead of condemnation.

A cruel God would rule through fear, not self-giving love. A controlling God would enforce compliance, not invite trust.

A volatile God would punish first, not delay judgment for mercy.

The cross only makes sense if God's justice is **not rooted in cruelty**, but in love that is willing to suffer for the sake of restoration.

This is the first major fault line in the modern accusation. One cannot simultaneously claim that the Bible presents an abusive God *and* that Jesus' crucifixion is meaningful. If God is abusive, the cross is not redemptive—it is monstrous.

Either the Bible fundamentally misrepresents God, or modern readers have fundamentally misread the Bible.

This book argues the latter.

Jesus and the Refusal to Coerce

One of the most emotionally revealing moments in the Gospels occurs not in a miracle, confrontation, or sermon, but in Jesus' grief.

As He approaches Jerusalem—the city that will soon reject Him, condemn Him, and hand Him over to be killed—Jesus speaks words that shatter the image of a coercive God:

"Jerusalem, Jerusalem, who kills the prophets and stones those who are sent to her! How often I wanted to gather your children together, like a hen gathers her chicks under her wings, and you would not!"
— **Gospel of Matthew 23:37 (WEB)**

This is not the voice of a tyrant.

Jesus does not threaten Jerusalem with immediate punishment. He does not override their will. He does not force repentance through power. Instead, He laments rejection. His desire is protective, nurturing, and voluntary—*"like a hen gathers her chicks."*

The tragedy, according to Jesus, is not that God rejected humanity, but that humanity rejected God.

This single moment dismantles the assumption that divine authority requires coercion. God's love, as presented here, respects human agency—even when that freedom leads to rejection, suffering, and loss.

A God who allows refusal is not seeking domination.
A God who grieves rejection is not indifferent.
A God who longs to gather rather than compel is not cruel.

If Scripture were primarily designed to control people, this passage would not exist.

Why the Accusation Persists

The belief that the Bible is outdated or harmful does not emerge in a vacuum. It often arises from very real wounds.

Throughout history, Scripture has been misused—sometimes deliberately—to justify violence, oppression, racism, misogyny, and fear-based religion. Entire systems of power have cloaked themselves in biblical language while betraying biblical values. For many, the harm associated with these abuses feels inseparable from the text itself.

But misuse does not define meaning.

In fact, one of the most overlooked features of the Bible is how frequently it **critiques human authority**, exposes religious hypocrisy, and warns against confusing power with righteousness. The Bible does not present a naive view of leadership; it assumes corruption is possible—even likely.

That Scripture contains internal warnings against injustice, abuse, and false authority is not evidence of manipulation. It is evidence of moral self-awareness.

The question, then, is not whether the Bible has been used to harm people—it has. The question is whether the Bible itself endorses that harm, or whether it repeatedly calls humanity back from it.

This book contends that Scripture's central message is not control, but **restoration**.

The Question That Must Be Faced

If the Bible truly teaches cruelty, then Jesus' death is either meaningless or immoral.
If God delights in domination, then the cross is unnecessary.
If justice is indistinguishable from power, then love is an illusion.

But if Jesus truly lived, taught, and died as the Gospels claim—then Scripture is not pointing humanity toward fear, but toward reconciliation.

This book is written for those willing to examine that claim honestly.

Not through inherited assumptions.
Not through fear-based religion.
Not through cultural caricatures.

But through Scripture itself.

Looking Ahead

The chapters that follow will explore a single, consistent claim woven throughout the Bible: **that justice does not come from power, status, or control—but from the character of God Himself.**

The next chapter begins where wisdom literature draws a sharp line:

Human power is not the same as divine justice.

"Many seek the ruler's favor,
but justice for man comes from the LORD."
— Proverbs 29:26 (WEB)

Human Nature vs. Divine Justice

Human societies have always been organized around power. Kings, judges, governments, religious leaders, institutions—every culture develops systems that determine who is heard, who is protected, and who is punished. Access to authority has often meant access to safety, provision, and justice. To be favored by those in power is to be secure; to fall out of favor is to be vulnerable.

The Bible does not deny this reality. In fact, it names it plainly.

"Many seek the ruler's favor,
but justice for man comes from Yahweh."
— **Book of Proverbs 29:26 (WEB)**

This single verse draws a sharp and uncomfortable distinction—one that many readers miss.

It does not say rulers are irrelevant.
It does not say authority is meaningless.
It does not say justice never passes through human systems.

It says something far more radical:

Justice does not originate with power.

The Human Instinct to Seek Favor

"Many seek the ruler's favor."
The proverb begins by acknowledging something deeply human.

People seek approval from those who hold influence because influence determines outcomes. Whether in ancient courts or modern institutions, favor opens doors. It grants protection. It tilts the scales. From job promotions to legal decisions to social acceptance, human systems often reward alignment with authority.

Scripture does not mock this instinct—it recognizes it. The problem is not that people seek favor. The problem is what happens when favor is mistaken for justice.

When justice becomes dependent on access, morality becomes negotiable. Truth becomes flexible. Righteousness becomes performative. What matters most is no longer what is right, but who is pleased.

Proverbs does not condemn rulers here. It **relativizes them**.

Human authority exists—but it is not ultimate.

Justice Does Not Flow Upward

The second half of Proverbs 29:26 overturns the entire assumption:

"But justice for man comes from Yahweh."

This is not poetic exaggeration. It is a theological claim.

Justice does not rise from institutions to God. Justice descends from God to institutions.

In other words, authority is accountable. Power does not define righteousness—righteousness judges power.

This distinction matters because human systems are capable of profound injustice while appearing legitimate. Courts can err. Leaders can corrupt. Religions can distort. History bears this out repeatedly.

The Bible does not pretend otherwise.

"Don't put your trust in princes,
in a son of man in whom there is no help."
— **Book of Psalms 146:3 (WEB)**

This is not cynicism—it is realism. Human beings are limited, fallible, and susceptible to self-interest. Justice rooted solely in power will always be unstable.

That is why Scripture insists justice must be grounded in **God's character**, not human authority.

What Kind of Justice Comes From God?

Here is where many readers go wrong.

When people hear "God's justice," they often imagine severity, punishment, or divine anger. But Proverbs does not define justice by consequences—it defines justice by **source**.

Justice "comes from Yahweh" because Yahweh's character determines what justice is.

Throughout Scripture, God repeatedly describes Himself not primarily as powerful, but as **patient, compassionate, and slow to anger**.

"Yahweh is merciful and gracious,
slow to anger, and abundant in loving kindness."
— Book of Psalms 103:8 (WEB)

This description appears again and again across the Bible. It is not incidental. It is foundational.

If justice comes from a God who is slow to anger, then justice itself must be **measured, restrained, and restorative**—not volatile or cruel.

Justice rooted in God's character seeks truth, not domination. It aims to set things right, not simply to punish wrong.

Authority Without Character Is Dangerous

The Bible's insistence that justice comes from God is not abstract theology—it is a safeguard.

When authority detaches itself from moral character, it becomes dangerous. History provides countless examples of regimes that claimed legitimacy while perpetrating injustice. Power alone cannot produce justice; it can only enforce outcomes.

This is why Scripture consistently critiques leaders—kings, priests, judges—when they confuse authority with righteousness.

"Woe to those who decree unrighteous decrees, and to the writers who write oppressive decrees."
— **Book of Isaiah 10:1 (WEB)**

The Bible does not baptize power. It **tests it**.

This is precisely what makes the accusation that Scripture exists to subjugate people so fragile. A text designed for control would not repeatedly undermine unchecked authority.

Jesus and the Exposure of False Justice

Jesus enters the world at a moment when religious and political power are tightly intertwined. The Roman state enforces order through violence, while religious leaders preserve authority through exclusion and fear.

Yet Jesus consistently refuses to align justice with power.

He heals on the Sabbath, not to provoke rebellion, but to reveal mercy.
He eats with sinners, not to ignore sin, but to restore people.
He challenges leaders, not to seize control, but to expose hypocrisy.

When Jesus is finally condemned, it is not because He is guilty, but because He threatens established power.

Human authorities judge Him guilty.
God overturns the verdict.

The resurrection is not merely a miracle—it is a declaration that **human judgment is not final**.

This is Proverbs 29:26 enacted in history.

Justice That Is For Humanity

The idea that God is against humanity collapses under this framework.

If justice flows from a God who is patient, merciful, and slow to anger, then justice is not designed to crush people—it is designed to **restore them**.

This is why the prophet Jeremiah records God's words to a displaced and fearful people:

"For I know the thoughts that I think toward you," says Yahweh,
"thoughts of peace, and not of evil,
to give you hope and a future."
— Book of Jeremiah 29:11 (WEB)

Justice that comes from such a God cannot be hostile by nature. It may confront wrongdoing, but it does so for the sake of healing, not destruction.

God's justice is not opposed to humanity—it is opposed to whatever deforms humanity.

Reframing the Question

The central question is not whether authority exists. It is whether authority reflects God's character.

Proverbs 29:26 does not invite rebellion—it invites **discernment**. It teaches readers to distinguish between access and righteousness, power and truth, influence and justice.

Human systems matter. But they are not ultimate. God is.

And if God is slow to anger, rich in mercy, and committed to restoration, then justice itself must be understood through that lens.

"Slow to Anger": The Most Repeated Description of God

If there is one phrase that consistently disrupts the idea of an angry, volatile God, it is this:

"Slow to anger."

It appears across the Bible with remarkable consistency—so often, in fact, that it becomes impossible to dismiss as incidental. This description is not tucked away in obscure passages or isolated to a single author or era. It appears in the Law, the Prophets, the Psalms, and is ultimately embodied in the life of Jesus.

The Bible does not primarily define God by power, wrath, or judgment. It defines Him by **restraint**.

This matters more than most readers realize.

God Tells Us Who He Is

In the ancient world, gods were typically described as volatile, easily offended, and quick to punish. Divine anger was assumed to be unpredictable, and human beings were expected to appease it through fear, ritual, or sacrifice.

The God of the Bible breaks from this pattern decisively.

One of the clearest self-descriptions of God appears when He speaks about Himself directly:

"Yahweh, Yahweh, a merciful and gracious God, slow to anger,
and abundant in loving kindness and truth."
— Book of Exodus 34:6 (WEB)

This moment is critical. God is not being described *by humans*—He is describing Himself. And the first moral attribute He emphasizes is not dominance, but mercy; not anger, but patience.

If Scripture were written to justify fear-based control, this would be a strange place to begin.

Slowness Is Not Weakness

Modern readers often confuse "slow to anger" with permissiveness or moral indifference. But biblically, slowness is not the absence of justice—it is the discipline of restraint.

To be slow to anger is to:

- Delay judgment
- Allow space for repentance
- Resist impulsive retaliation
- Prioritize restoration over retribution

This is not weakness. It is moral strength.

The Psalms repeat this truth explicitly:

"Yahweh is merciful and gracious,
slow to anger, and abundant in loving kindness."
— **Book of Psalms 103:8 (WEB)**

What follows in the same psalm is just as important:

"He will not always accuse;
neither will he stay angry forever.
He has not dealt with us according to our sins,
nor repaid us for our iniquities."
— Psalm 103:9–10 (WEB)

Here, anger is acknowledged—but it is explicitly **limited**. God's anger is not His default posture. It is restrained, purposeful, and temporary.

If justice flows from God's character, then justice itself must reflect this restraint.

Why This Description Is Repeated

Scripture repeats "slow to anger" because humans repeatedly assume the opposite.

When people suffer, they often conclude that God is angry. When judgment occurs, they assume God delights in punishment. When moral boundaries exist, they infer hostility toward freedom.

The Bible corrects this assumption again and again.

"For the Lord will not cast off forever.
For though he causes grief, yet he will have compassion

according to the multitude of his loving kindnesses.
For he does not afflict willingly,
nor grieve the children of men."
— Book of Lamentations 3:31–33 (WEB)

This passage does not deny suffering. It denies *intentional cruelty*. God does not afflict "willingly"— that is, suffering is not His desire or delight.

Justice may involve correction, but correction is not the same as cruelty.

God's Patience Is Oriented Toward Life

The prophets make this explicit. When God confronts wrongdoing, He explains why His anger is restrained:

"Have I any pleasure in the death of the wicked?"
says the Lord Yahweh;
"and not rather that he should return from his way, and live?"
— Book of Ezekiel 18:23 (WEB)

This is one of the clearest statements of divine intent in all of Scripture. God does not take pleasure in punishment. His desire is repentance and life.

The same truth is repeated later:

"I have no pleasure in the death of the wicked; but that the wicked turn from his way and live."
— Ezekiel 33:11 (WEB)

Justice that comes from such a God cannot be fundamentally hostile to humanity. It is corrective, not destructive.

Jesus as "Slow to Anger" in Flesh and Blood

Jesus does not merely teach patience—He embodies it.

Throughout the Gospels, Jesus encounters:

- Hypocrisy
- Betrayal
- Ignorance
- Rejection
- Injustice

And yet, He consistently responds with restraint.

He warns before judging.
He invites before condemning.
He forgives while being wronged.

Even at the cross—where injustice reaches its peak—Jesus does not lash out.

"Father, forgive them, for they don't know what they are doing."
— Gospel of Luke 23:34 (WEB)

This is "slow to anger" made visible.

If God were eager to punish, the cross would have been the moment. Instead, it becomes the place where mercy absorbs injustice.

Slowness Does Not Eliminate Judgment

The Bible does not deny judgment—it reframes it.

Judgment exists because justice matters. But judgment is never presented as God's delight. It is presented as a tragic necessity when restoration is refused.

This is why Scripture consistently places **patience before judgment**.

The New Testament echoes this clearly:

"Or do you despise the riches of his goodness, forbearance, and patience, not knowing that the goodness of God leads you to repentance?"
— **Epistle to the Romans 2:4 (WEB)**

God's patience is not moral indifference—it is an invitation.

Why This Changes Everything

If God is slow to anger, then:

- Justice is not impulsive

- Judgment is not arbitrary
- Authority is not abusive
- Power is accountable to love

This dismantles the claim that the Bible presents a cruel God. A God who repeatedly delays anger, invites repentance, and prioritizes life is not seeking to subjugate humanity.

He is seeking to restore it.

This also reframes obedience. Obedience is not submission to fear—it is trust in a God whose character has proven worthy.

Returning to the Central Claim

Proverbs 29:26 told us that justice comes from God, not rulers. This chapter tells us **why that justice can be trusted**.

It flows from a God who is:

- Merciful
- Patient
- Slow to anger
- Focused on restoration

This is not a marginal theme. It is the backbone of Scripture.

Justice as Restoration, Not Retribution

For many people, the word *justice* immediately evokes punishment. To be just, they assume, is to retaliate. Wrong must be met with consequence; offense must be answered with force. In this framework, justice is measured by severity, and fairness is defined by proportional pain.

This assumption shapes how many read the Bible. When Scripture speaks of judgment, it is often interpreted as evidence that God is harsh, vindictive, or eager to punish. Divine justice becomes indistinguishable from retribution, and God is imagined as a cosmic enforcer whose primary concern is settling scores.

But the Bible itself does not define justice this way.

From its earliest texts to its final pages, Scripture consistently presents justice not as vengeance for its own sake, but as **the work of restoring what has been broken**. Punishment may appear within that process, but it is never the goal. Restoration is.

This distinction is critical—because a retributive God would be against humanity, while a restorative God is unmistakably for it.

What Biblical Justice Actually Means

In the Hebrew Scriptures, the word most often translated as *justice* is *mishpat*. While it includes judgment and accountability, its meaning is far broader than punishment. *Mishpat* refers to right order, moral balance, and the correction of what has gone wrong so that life can flourish again.

Justice, in this sense, is not primarily about inflicting pain on the guilty. It is about **setting things right**.

This is why biblical justice is frequently paired with compassion, mercy, and care for the vulnerable. The prophets do not accuse Israel of lacking punishment—they accuse Israel of lacking justice for the poor, the oppressed, and the forgotten.

"What does Yahweh require of you,
but to do justice,
to love kindness,
and to walk humbly with your God?"
— **Book of Micah 6:8 (WEB)**

Justice and kindness are not opposites here—they are inseparable. Any understanding of justice that excludes mercy is already a distortion.

God's Own Testimony About Judgment

The clearest way to understand biblical justice is to listen to what God Himself says about it.

Through the prophet Ezekiel, God directly confronts the assumption that He delights in punishment:

"Have I any pleasure in the death of the wicked?" says the Lord Yahweh;
"and not rather that he should return from his way, and live?"
— **Book of Ezekiel 18:23 (WEB)**

This question is rhetorical—and devastating to the caricature of a cruel God. God explicitly denies pleasure in destruction. His desire is repentance and life.

Later, God repeats the same truth, leaving no room for misunderstanding:

"I have no pleasure in the death of the wicked, but that the wicked turn from his way and live."
— Ezekiel 33:11 (WEB)

If justice comes from a God who does not delight in punishment, then justice itself cannot be fundamentally punitive.

Judgment exists, but it exists **for the sake of life**, not for the satisfaction of wrath.

Why Punishment Still Appears in Scripture

This raises an important question. If God's justice is restorative, why does Scripture contain warnings, consequences, and moments of judgment?

The answer lies in purpose.

Correction is not the same as cruelty. Accountability is not the same as vengeance. A surgeon may cut in order to heal; a parent may discipline in order to protect. The presence of pain does not define the motive.

The Bible consistently presents judgment as **reluctant**, **measured**, and **responsive to human choice**—never arbitrary or impulsive.

This is why the book of Lamentations, written in the aftermath of devastation, can still say:

"For the Lord will not cast off forever.
For though he causes grief, yet he will have compassion
according to the multitude of his loving kindnesses.
For he does not afflict willingly,
nor grieve the children of men."
— **Book of Lamentations 3:31–33 (WEB)**

Justice may involve grief—but grief is not God's desire. Compassion is.

A God who disciplines unwillingly is not seeking to destroy. He is seeking to restore what refuses correction by gentler means.

Retribution Ends Stories; Restoration Continues Them

Retributive justice closes the book. It says, "You are defined by your worst act, and there is nothing more to be done."

Restorative justice keeps the story open. It says, "Something is broken—but it can still be healed."

Scripture overwhelmingly favors the second vision.

Time and again, God confronts wrongdoing not with immediate annihilation, but with warnings, patience, and calls to return. Judgment comes only when restoration is persistently refused—and even then, it is framed as tragic, not triumphant.

This is why the Bible so often portrays God as pleading, waiting, and relenting.

"Yahweh is gracious and merciful,
slow to anger, and of great loving kindness.
Yahweh is good to all.
His tender mercies are over all his works."
— **Book of Psalms 145:8–9 (WEB)**

A God whose mercy extends "over all his works" is not building a system designed to crush humanity.

Jesus and the Fulfillment of Restorative Justice

Jesus does not replace Old Testament justice—He fulfills it.

Throughout His ministry, Jesus consistently chooses restoration over retribution. He forgives sinners before they reform. He heals before demanding obedience. He restores dignity before addressing behavior.

When religious leaders demand punishment, Jesus responds with mercy—not because justice does not matter, but because **restoration matters more**.

Even at the cross, where justice and injustice collide, Jesus does not retaliate.

"Father, forgive them, for they don't know what they are doing."
— **Gospel of Luke 23:34 (WEB)**

This is not justice abandoned—it is justice transformed. The cross becomes the place where wrongdoing is taken seriously enough to be absorbed, not ignored or returned.

Retribution would have ended the story.
Restoration opened the door to resurrection.

Justice That Serves Love

If justice is divorced from love, it becomes tyranny. If love is divorced from justice, it becomes sentimentality. Scripture refuses both extremes.

Biblical justice serves love by confronting what destroys it.

This is why the Bible can say, without contradiction:

"Yahweh loves righteousness and justice."
— **Book of Psalms 33:5 (WEB)**

God loves justice because He loves what justice protects: life, dignity, truth, and relationship.

Justice is not God's weapon against humanity—it is His instrument for humanity's healing.

Re-centering the Narrative

The accusation that the Bible promotes cruelty collapses here. A text centered on restoration cannot be fundamentally oppressive. A God who prefers repentance to punishment cannot be hostile by nature.

This does not eliminate accountability. It reframes it.

God is against sin because sin deforms humanity.
God is against injustice because injustice destroys the vulnerable.
God is against evil because evil corrodes life.

But God is **for people**.

That is why justice comes from Him—and not from rulers.

The Beatitudes: Justice Turned Upside Down

When Jesus begins His public teaching, He does not start with commands, warnings, or threats. He does not outline a legal code, establish a hierarchy, or appeal to fear. Instead, He pronounces blessings—statements of favor—on people the world does not consider powerful, successful, or secure.

This alone should give us pause.

The Beatitudes are often treated as gentle spiritual poetry—comforting but impractical, idealistic but unrealistic. In reality, they are a **direct challenge to power-based systems of justice**. Jesus is not offering vague encouragement; He is redefining who stands within God's favor and what true justice looks like.

If Proverbs 29:26 draws a line between human power and divine justice, the Beatitudes show us what justice looks like when that line is taken seriously.

A New Starting Point for Justice

Jesus opens the Sermon on the Mount with these words:

"Blessed are the poor in spirit,
for theirs is the Kingdom of Heaven."
— **Gospel of Matthew 5:3 (WEB)**

This is not accidental. In human systems, blessing flows toward strength, confidence, and success. Jesus begins with poverty—not economic poverty alone, but spiritual humility. Those who recognize their need, their dependence, their lack of self-sufficiency, are the ones He calls blessed.

Justice, in Jesus' framework, does not reward self-assertion. It responds to humility.

This immediately overturns the assumption that God's favor mirrors human hierarchies. Divine justice begins where human power systems usually end.

Meekness as Moral Strength

Few Beatitudes are more misunderstood than this one:

"Blessed are the meek,
for they shall inherit the earth."
— Matthew 5:5 (WEB)

Meekness is often mistaken for weakness. But biblically, meekness refers to **strength under control**—the disciplined refusal to dominate, retaliate, or coerce.

In other words, meekness is the opposite of abusive power.

Jesus does not say the aggressive will inherit the earth, or that the ruthless will shape the future. He says those who refuse to use power destructively are the ones aligned with God's justice.

A God who blesses meekness is not training people for domination. He is shaping them for restoration.

Mercy at the Center of Justice

Jesus continues:

"Blessed are the merciful,
for they shall obtain mercy."
— Matthew 5:7 (WEB)

This statement directly challenges retributive justice. Mercy is not the suspension of justice—it is justice shaped by compassion.

Mercy acknowledges wrongdoing but refuses to define people by their worst failures. It seeks healing rather than humiliation. It aims to restore relationship rather than assert superiority.

If God's justice were primarily punitive, mercy would undermine it. But Jesus presents mercy as **the fulfillment of justice**, not its enemy.

This aligns perfectly with what we have already seen: God is slow to anger, patient, and oriented toward repentance and life. The Beatitudes do not soften justice—they **reveal its true purpose**.

Righteousness Without Cruelty

Jesus blesses those who hunger and thirst for righteousness:

"Blessed are those who hunger and thirst after righteousness,
for they shall be filled."
— Matthew 5:6 (WEB)

Righteousness here is not moral superiority or rule enforcement. It is a longing for things to be set right—for truth, integrity, and justice to prevail.

This hunger assumes something is wrong with the world—but it does not assume cruelty is the solution.

Jesus never blesses those who enforce righteousness through fear. He blesses those who *long* for it deeply and are willing to be shaped by God rather than impose themselves on others.

Justice driven by hunger for righteousness is very different from justice driven by desire for control.

Peacemaking as Active Justice

Perhaps the most misunderstood Beatitude is this:

"Blessed are the peacemakers,
for they shall be called children of God."
— Matthew 5:9 (WEB)

Peacemaking is not passivity. It is not conflict avoidance. It is not silence in the face of injustice.

Peacemaking is **active reconciliation**. It requires confronting wrongdoing, naming truth, and working toward restored relationship. It is costly. It demands humility, patience, and courage.

Only a God who values restoration over domination would elevate peacemaking to such a place of honor.

Peacemakers are called "children of God" because they reflect God's character. Justice that seeks peace rather than victory mirrors the heart of a God who is for humanity.

The Blessedness of the Vulnerable

The Beatitudes repeatedly bless those who are vulnerable:

- Those who mourn
- Those who are persecuted
- Those who suffer for righteousness

"Blessed are those who have been persecuted for righteousness' sake,
for theirs is the Kingdom of Heaven."
— Matthew 5:10 (WEB)

In human systems, persecution is often seen as failure. In Jesus' framework, it becomes evidence of alignment with God's justice.

This does not glorify suffering—but it exposes the lie that power determines truth.

God's justice does not always protect people from harm in the short term, but it **vindicates them in the long term**. That is why justice comes from God, not rulers.

The Beatitudes and the Character of God

Taken together, the Beatitudes reveal a consistent picture:

- Justice rooted in humility
- Strength expressed through restraint
- Righteousness pursued without cruelty
- Mercy elevated above retaliation
- Peace valued over domination

This is not a new ethic disconnected from the rest of Scripture. It is the **full expression of the God who is slow to anger**, merciful, and committed to restoration.

Jesus does not contradict the Old Testament vision of God—He clarifies it.

Why This Undermines the "Harmful Bible" Claim

A text designed to control people would not:

- Bless the powerless
- Elevate meekness

- Center mercy
- Honor peacemaking
- Validate the persecuted

The Beatitudes are deeply subversive. They dismantle fear-based religion and expose power-driven righteousness as hollow.

They reveal a God whose justice does not crush people into obedience, but **forms them into reflectors of His character**.

Re-centering Justice Once More

Justice, as Jesus defines it, is not about winning. It is about restoring what is broken. It is not about enforcing dominance. It is about aligning human life with God's love.

This is why the Beatitudes belong in this book. They show us that the God of Scripture is not against humanity. He is reshaping humanity—patiently, gently, and faithfully.

"How Often I Wanted to Gather You": Love Without Coercion

There are moments in Scripture where theology is not argued but **revealed through emotion**. Where the heart of God is not explained in doctrine, but exposed through grief. One such moment occurs near the end of Jesus' public ministry, as He approaches Jerusalem—the city that will soon reject Him, condemn Him, and hand Him over to be crucified.

Jesus does not respond with anger.
He does not issue threats.
He does not assert power.

He weeps.

"Jerusalem, Jerusalem, who kills the prophets and stones those who are sent to her! How often I wanted to gather your children together, like a hen gathers her chicks under her wings, and you would not!"
— **Gospel of Matthew 23:37 (WEB)**

This single verse dismantles one of the most persistent misconceptions about God: that divine authority must operate through force.

A God Who Wants—but Does Not Force

Jesus' words are striking for what they *do not* say.

He does not say, *"I gathered you."*
He says, *"I wanted to."*

He does not say, *"You were unable."*
He says, *"You would not."*

This distinction is crucial. Jesus portrays God not as overpowering human will, but as **respecting it—even when that will leads to tragedy**.

Love that coerces is not love. Justice that overrides agency is not justice. The God revealed in Jesus refuses both.

This is not weakness. It is restraint born of love.

A God who allows rejection is not indifferent; He is honoring the dignity of human choice.

The Metaphor That Changes Everything

Jesus chooses an unexpected image: a hen gathering her chicks.

Not a king commanding subjects.
Not a judge issuing sentences.
Not a warrior enforcing loyalty.

A mother protecting her young.

This metaphor communicates vulnerability, care, and self-giving protection. A hen does not dominate her chicks—she shelters them, even at risk to herself.

This is how Jesus describes God.

If Scripture were designed to promote domination or subjugation, this image would be inexplicable. It does not inspire fear. It invites trust.

God's desire, according to Jesus, is not control—but **closeness**.

Rejection Does Not Cancel Love

Jerusalem's history is one of resistance. Jesus acknowledges this openly: *"who kills the prophets and stones those who are sent to her."* God has been reaching out repeatedly—and repeatedly refused.

Yet Jesus does not say, *"I stopped wanting."*

"How often I wanted…"

The persistence of that desire reveals something essential about God's character. Rejection does not harden His heart. It grieves Him.

This stands in sharp contrast to human power systems, which often respond to resistance with escalation. When authority is challenged, force is applied. When control is threatened, punishment follows.

God does the opposite.

He continues to invite—even knowing rejection is likely.

Why Coercion Would Undermine the Cross

If God's primary goal were obedience at any cost, the cross would be unnecessary.

Force could have accomplished submission.
Fear could have enforced compliance.
Power could have silenced resistance.

Instead, God chooses the most vulnerable path imaginable.

Jesus does not compel belief. He absorbs rejection. He does not crush rebellion. He suffers under it.

This makes sense only if God values **relationship over control**.

The cross is not God overpowering humanity—it is God allowing humanity to do its worst, and responding with forgiveness.

"Father, forgive them, for they don't know what they are doing."
— **Gospel of Luke 23:34 (WEB)**

A coercive God would never pray this prayer.

Divine Authority That Refuses to Dominate

The refusal to coerce is not an isolated theme. It runs throughout Jesus' ministry.

- He invites disciples to follow—He does not conscript them.
- He allows people to walk away—rich rulers included.
- He asks questions instead of issuing commands.
- He warns of consequences but never forces compliance.

This reveals a form of authority that is profoundly unsettling to power-driven systems. Jesus exercises authority without domination. He speaks truth without violence. He corrects without humiliation.

This is what divine authority looks like when justice flows from character rather than power.

Why This Matters for the "Harmful Bible" Claim

One of the strongest modern accusations against the Bible is that it promotes forced belief and suppresses dissent. But the God revealed in Jesus consistently does the opposite.

He persuades rather than coerces.
He invites rather than compels.
He grieves rather than retaliates.

A God who refuses to force obedience cannot be accused of seeking subjugation as His primary goal.

That accusation collapses under Jesus' own words.

Love That Allows Loss

There is a cost to love without coercion. It allows rejection. It allows suffering. It allows loss.

Jesus knows Jerusalem will reject Him. He knows the consequences will be devastating. Yet He does not override their will.

This tells us something difficult but necessary: **God's love values freedom even when freedom is misused**.

A God who is for humanity does not treat people as objects to be controlled. He treats them as persons to be loved—even when that love is refused.

Justice, Love, and Patience Converge

This moment in Matthew 23 brings together everything we have seen so far:

- Justice that is restorative, not retributive
- A God who is slow to anger
- Authority grounded in character
- Love that refuses coercion

It confirms again that God's justice is trustworthy precisely because it is shaped by love.

God does not force humanity back into His care. He calls, invites, waits, and—when necessary—suffers.

This is not the posture of an enemy.

Love Is Not Easily Angered: Paul and the Shape of Divine Love

Few passages of Scripture are quoted more often—and understood less—than Paul's description of love in First Corinthians. It is read at weddings, stitched into artwork, and recited as poetry. But stripped of its context, it is often reduced to sentiment rather than truth.

Paul was not writing about romance.
He was not offering idealistic advice.
He was describing **the very nature of God**.

When Paul defines love, he is not inventing a new ethic. He is articulating, with precision, the same divine character revealed in the Law, the Prophets, and ultimately in Jesus Christ.

This is especially clear in one often-overlooked phrase:

Love is not easily angered.

Love as God's Moral Core

Paul writes:

"Love is patient and is kind; love doesn't envy. Love doesn't brag, is not proud, doesn't behave itself improperly, doesn't seek its own way, is not provoked, takes no account of evil."
— **First Epistle to the Corinthians 13:4–5 (WEB)**

Paul's words echo unmistakably with the Old Testament description of God as "slow to anger." This is not coincidence. Paul is drawing directly from Israel's understanding of God's character.

To say that love is "not easily angered" is to say that love:

- Exercises restraint
- Refuses impulsive retaliation
- Prioritizes restoration over reaction
- Absorbs offense rather than escalating conflict

This is not weakness. It is **disciplined strength**.

A love that explodes at provocation is not love—it is insecurity.

Paul Is Describing God, Not Merely Behavior

Paul is not giving abstract advice on how humans *should* behave in ideal circumstances. He is explaining how love operates because **God Himself operates this way**.

Elsewhere, Paul states this directly:

"God demonstrates his own love toward us, in that while we were yet sinners, Christ died for us."
— **Epistle to the Romans 5:8 (WEB)**

This is love that acts *before* repentance. Love that absorbs wrongdoing instead of returning it. Love that delays anger not because sin is insignificant, but because people matter.

Paul's definition of love aligns perfectly with the God revealed in Jesus—a God who waits, invites, forgives, and restores.

"Not Provoked" and the Refusal to Escalate

The phrase translated "not easily angered" can also be rendered "not provoked." This matters because provocation assumes offense.

Love does not deny offense.
Love refuses to let offense control its response.

This reframes divine justice completely. God does not respond to human failure with immediate wrath. He does not retaliate reflexively. He does not escalate rebellion into annihilation.

Instead, He waits.

"Or do you despise the riches of his goodness, forbearance, and patience, not knowing that the goodness of God leads you to repentance?"
— **Epistle to the Romans 2:4 (WEB)**

Paul makes the logic explicit: **God's patience is purposeful**. It exists to create space for repentance and restoration.

This is justice shaped by love.

Love That Keeps No Record of Wrongs

Paul continues:

"Love... takes no account of evil."
— 1 Corinthians 13:5 (WEB)

This does not mean love ignores wrongdoing. It means love refuses to keep score in order to justify vengeance.

A justice system obsessed with records and tallies inevitably becomes punitive. A justice system shaped by love seeks healing rather than humiliation.

This is why Scripture consistently portrays God as forgiving rather than vindictive.

"As far as the east is from the west,
so far has he removed our transgressions from us."
— **Book of Psalms 103:12 (WEB)**

God does not erase accountability—but He refuses to define people by their worst acts.

Love, Justice, and the Cross

Paul's definition of love only makes sense in light of the cross.

At the cross, God does not retaliate against humanity's violence. He absorbs it. He does not return insult for insult or suffering for suffering. He responds with forgiveness.

This is not the suspension of justice—it is justice fulfilled through love.

Retribution would have ended the story.
Love opened the door to resurrection.

If the Bible were a tool of domination, the cross would be a display of power. Instead, it is a display of **self-giving restraint**.

Why This Refutes the "Angry God" Narrative

The accusation that the Bible presents an angry, volatile God collapses when examined alongside Paul's theology.

Paul's God:

- Is patient
- Is kind
- Is not provoked
- Keeps no record of wrongs
- Absorbs injustice to restore relationship

This is not a God eager to punish. This is a God eager to save.

If Paul's definition of love is true—and Scripture insists it is—then God's justice cannot be rooted in cruelty. It must be grounded in patience, mercy, and restorative intent.

Love as the Measure of True Justice

Paul ends his description of love with a sweeping statement:

"Love bears all things, believes all things, hopes all things, endures all things."
— 1 Corinthians 13:7 (WEB)

This is not naïveté. It is **resilient commitment**.

Love endures because it is invested in restoration. It refuses to abandon people at their worst. It does not weaponize anger or rush to condemnation.

This is why justice that comes from God is trustworthy. It flows from love that is slow to anger and committed to healing.

Re-centering the Argument

We have now seen this truth from multiple angles:

- God describes Himself as slow to anger

- Jesus embodies restraint and mercy
- Paul defines love as patient and unprovoked

There is no contradiction. There is consistency.

The Bible does not present an angry God barely holding back rage. It presents a God **holding back judgment** for the sake of love.

God is not against humanity.
He is for it—patiently, persistently, and at great personal cost.

The Cross: Where Justice and Love Meet

If there is one place where the accusation of an angry, cruel God seems strongest, it is the cross.

For many critics, the crucifixion appears to confirm their worst suspicions: divine wrath poured out on an innocent victim, violence framed as justice, suffering demanded to satisfy anger. From this perspective, the cross becomes either barbaric or manipulative—a religious symbol used to normalize abuse and call it salvation.

If that reading is correct, Christianity is not good news.
It is moral confusion at best, and spiritual violence at worst.

But Scripture itself does not interpret the cross that way.

In fact, when the Bible explains the meaning of the cross, it consistently rejects the idea that God's primary motivation is anger. Instead, the cross is presented as the place where **justice and love converge**, not collide.

The Cross Was Not God vs. Jesus

One of the most common misunderstandings of the crucifixion is the idea that God the Father is angry, and Jesus steps in to absorb that anger on humanity's behalf—as if the Trinity were divided against itself.

The New Testament never presents the cross this way.

Instead, Scripture insists that **God Himself is acting in love through Christ**.

"God was in Christ, reconciling the world to himself, not counting their trespasses against them."
— **Second Epistle to the Corinthians 5:19 (WEB)**

This verse dismantles the notion of divine internal conflict. God is not punishing Jesus instead of humanity. God is **entering human suffering** to reconcile humanity to Himself.

The cross is not God acting *against* Jesus.
It is God acting *for* humanity.

Justice Is Taken Seriously—But Not Violently Returned

The cross does not deny the seriousness of evil. Scripture never minimizes wrongdoing, injustice, or human violence. What it denies is that evil must be overcome by returning violence with violence.

At the cross, injustice is fully exposed:

- Religious leaders abuse authority
- Political power condemns the innocent
- Crowds choose fear over truth
- Violence silences righteousness

And yet, God does not respond by crushing His enemies.

He absorbs the injustice.

"He was pierced for our transgressions.
He was crushed for our iniquities.
The punishment that brought our peace was on him;
and by his wounds we are healed."
— **Book of Isaiah 53:5 (WEB)**

This is not retribution—it is **substitutionary restoration**. Violence is not returned; it is transformed.

Justice is satisfied not because someone suffers, but because **evil is confronted and undone through love**.

"Father, Forgive Them" and the End of Retribution

Perhaps the clearest revelation of the cross's meaning comes from Jesus' own words as He hangs dying:

"Father, forgive them, for they don't know what they are doing."
— **Gospel of Luke 23:34 (WEB)**

These words do not fit a narrative of divine rage. They fit a narrative of restrained, restorative justice.

Jesus does not deny wrongdoing.
He does not excuse injustice.
He names ignorance—but responds with forgiveness.

If the cross were primarily about satisfying anger, this prayer would be impossible.

Instead, the cross becomes the moment where God demonstrates what justice looks like when shaped by love: **truth without retaliation, accountability without annihilation, mercy without denial of evil**.

Love Initiates the Cross

The New Testament is explicit about what motivates the cross.

"For God so loved the world, that he gave his one and only Son…"
— **Gospel of John 3:16 (WEB)**

"God demonstrates his own love toward us, in that while we were yet sinners, Christ died for us."
— **Epistle to the Romans 5:8 (WEB)**

Love does not respond after repentance.
Love initiates reconciliation.

This matters because it means the cross is not God's reaction to human goodness—it is God's response to human brokenness.

A God who acts in love *before* repentance is not seeking control. He is seeking restoration.

Justice Without Love Would Have Ended the Story

If justice were only retributive, the cross would not exist.

Humanity would simply be condemned.
Wrong would be punished.
The story would end.

Instead, God chooses a path that preserves both justice *and* mercy.

"Mercy and truth meet together.
Righteousness and peace have kissed each other."
— Book of Psalms 85:10 (WEB)

The cross is where justice is upheld—evil is named, sin is confronted—but love determines the outcome.

Restoration, not destruction, becomes the final word.

The Cross as the Fulfillment of Proverbs 29:26

Everything we have examined so far converges here.

- Human rulers judged Jesus guilty

- Religious authorities condemned Him
- Political power executed Him

But justice did not come from rulers.

Justice came from God.

God overturned the verdict—not by violence, but by resurrection.

The resurrection is God's declaration that **human judgment is not final**, and that justice rooted in love ultimately triumphs.

Why the Cross Proves God Is For Humanity

A God who is against humanity would:

- Enforce obedience through fear
- Punish rebellion immediately
- Preserve power at all costs

The God revealed at the cross does the opposite.

He relinquishes power.
He absorbs suffering.
He forgives enemies.
He restores relationship.

This is not the posture of an enemy.

The cross proves that God is not standing over humanity in judgment, but **standing with humanity in suffering**.

Re-centering the Meaning of Salvation

Salvation is not rescue *from* God—it is rescue *by* God.

The cross does not protect humanity from God's anger.
It reveals God's love confronting evil without becoming evil.

This reframing changes everything:

- Faith becomes trust, not terror
- Obedience becomes response, not coercion
- Justice becomes healing, not revenge

God is not against humanity.
He is against whatever destroys humanity.

Resurrection: God's Verdict on Humanity

If the cross reveals the heart of God, the resurrection reveals His verdict.

The crucifixion exposes what human systems do when threatened by truth. Power protects itself. Authority silences disruption. Innocence is sacrificed for stability. Jesus is judged guilty by rulers, condemned by religious leaders, and executed by the state.

If the story ended there, the accusation that justice belongs to those in power would stand unchallenged.

But the story does not end there.

The resurrection is God's response—not only to Jesus' death, but to **every human verdict rooted in fear, control, and injustice**.

The Resurrection Is Not a Consolation Prize

The resurrection is often treated as an emotional comfort—proof that death is not the end, or that suffering will eventually be reversed. While it offers hope, it is far more than reassurance.

The resurrection is a **judgment**.

It is God's declaration that the verdict rendered by human authority was wrong.

"This Jesus God raised up, to which we all are witnesses."
— **Acts of the Apostles 2:32 (WEB)**

God does not negotiate with the verdict of the courts. He overturns it.

Human systems said, *"This man deserves death."*
God said, *"This is my Son."*

Justice does not come from rulers.
Justice comes from God.

Vindication, Not Retaliation

Notice what God does *not* do in the resurrection.

He does not destroy Jerusalem.
He does not overthrow Rome.
He does not retaliate against those responsible.

Instead, He raises Jesus.

This matters deeply. A God motivated by vengeance would have responded with force. A God motivated by domination would have responded with judgment. A God motivated by fear would have responded with terror.

God responds with **vindication**.

The resurrection declares that truth does not need violence to prevail. Love does not need coercion to win. Justice does not require retaliation to be fulfilled.

The Resurrection Confirms the Meaning of the Cross

Without the resurrection, the cross could be interpreted as failure. With the resurrection, the cross is revealed as faithfulness.

Paul makes this explicit:

"If Christ has not been raised, your faith is vain; you are still in your sins."
— **First Epistle to the Corinthians 15:17 (WEB)**

The resurrection confirms that the cross was not the defeat of love, but its victory.

God does not rescue Jesus *from* the cross.
He vindicates Him *through* it.

This distinction is crucial. It means suffering is not glorified—but it is not final. Evil is not ignored—but it does not win.

God's Verdict on Jesus Is God's Verdict on Humanity

The resurrection is not only about Jesus. It is about what God says concerning humanity itself.

Paul writes:

"But God, being rich in mercy, because of his great love with which he loved us… made us alive together with Christ."
— Epistle to the Ephesians 2:4–5 (WEB)

God's act of raising Jesus is the template for His intention toward humanity. Resurrection is not a private miracle—it is a public declaration of God's redemptive purpose.

Humanity is not discarded.
Humanity is restored.

A God who raises the crucified is not against people. He is **for their renewal**.

Justice Without Fear

The resurrection removes fear from justice.

If death—the ultimate tool of coercion—has been defeated, then fear loses its power to control. This is why the earliest Christian proclamation is not "Obey," but "He is risen."

Fear-based religion collapses in the face of resurrection. If God's final word is life, then obedience is no longer submission to threat—it is response to grace.

"There is therefore now no condemnation to those who are in Christ Jesus."
— **Epistle to the Romans 8:1 (WEB)**

Condemnation is not the driving force of God's justice. Restoration is.

Resurrection as the Answer to Power

Rome crucified Jesus to demonstrate authority. The resurrection exposes the limits of that authority.

The most powerful empire of the ancient world could kill—but it could not define reality.

The resurrection declares that **power does not get the final word**. Justice does not belong to those who control the present; it belongs to the God who restores the future.

This fulfills Proverbs 29:26 not as theory, but as history.

Why the Resurrection Matters for This Book's Claim

If God were against humanity, resurrection would be unnecessary. Judgment would suffice. If God were indifferent, the cross would be meaningless. If God were cruel, love would be expendable.

Instead, God raises Jesus—and in doing so, affirms the worth of human life, the dignity of suffering, and the possibility of renewal.

The resurrection says:

- Love was not naïve
- Mercy was not misplaced
- Justice was not compromised

It was fulfilled.

Resurrection as Invitation, Not Threat

God does not wield resurrection as leverage. He does not say, "Believe or else." He announces, "Life is possible."

The risen Christ appears not with condemnation, but with peace.

"Peace be to you."
— **Gospel of John 20:19 (WEB)**

This is the tone of divine justice after resurrection: peace offered, not demanded.

Re-centering the Narrative Once More

The resurrection confirms everything we have seen so far:

- God is slow to anger

- Justice is restorative
- Love refuses coercion
- Power does not define truth
- Humanity is not abandoned

God's verdict is not death.
God's verdict is life.

Faith Without Fear: Living Under Restorative Justice

If God's justice is restorative rather than retributive, and if love—not fear—is the engine of that justice, then faith itself must be re-examined.

Much of what people experience as "religion" is driven by fear: fear of punishment, fear of rejection, fear of getting it wrong. For many, faith becomes a constant calculation—*Am I doing enough? Am I safe? Am I one mistake away from condemnation?*

But fear-based faith is incompatible with everything we have seen so far.

A God who is slow to anger, who refuses coercion, who absorbs injustice at the cross, and who raises the crucified in love cannot be rightly approached through terror. Such a God invites trust, not panic.

This chapter asks a simple but unsettling question:

What does faith look like when fear is no longer the motivator?

The Difference Between Obedience and Submission

Fear-based religion often confuses obedience with submission.

Submission says, *"I comply because I must."*
Obedience says, *"I respond because I trust."*

Scripture consistently favors the second.

The apostle John states this plainly:

"There is no fear in love; but perfect love casts out fear, because fear has punishment. He who fears is not made perfect in love."
— **First Epistle of John 4:18 (WEB)**

This verse does not say fear is understandable. It says fear is **incompatible with love**.

If faith is driven primarily by fear of punishment, it is not yet aligned with God's character. Fear-based obedience may produce compliance, but it cannot produce transformation.

God is not looking for controlled behavior.
He is looking for restored relationship.

Authority Reframed: Power Accountable to Love

One of the most practical implications of restorative justice is how it reshapes authority.

In fear-based systems, authority exists to enforce compliance. Questioning authority is rebellion. Doubt is disloyalty. Power is protected, not examined.

Scripture does not operate this way.

Because justice comes from God—not rulers—authority is **accountable to God's character**. Leaders are judged by how well they reflect mercy, patience, humility, and truth.

Jesus makes this explicit:

"You know that the rulers of the nations lord it over them, and their great ones exercise authority over them. It shall not be so among you."
— Gospel of Matthew 20:25–26 (WEB)

Authority under God is not domination. It is service.

This has profound implications for churches, families, institutions, and personal leadership. Any authority that relies on fear to maintain control has already departed from the justice that comes from God.

Conscience Without Terror

Fear-based religion trains people to distrust their conscience. Moral reasoning becomes dangerous. Questions become threats. Silence becomes safety.

But Scripture consistently invites reflection, discernment, and growth.

Paul writes:

"For freedom Christ has set us free. Stand firm therefore, and don't be entangled again with a yoke of bondage."
— Epistle to the Galatians 5:1 (WEB)

Freedom here is not license—it is liberation from fear-driven control.

A conscience shaped by love does not need terror to guide it. It is sensitive to truth, responsive to correction, and oriented toward growth rather than self-protection.

God does not lead His people by intimidation. He leads them by invitation.

Repentance as Return, Not Groveling

Fear distorts repentance.

In fear-based systems, repentance becomes humiliation—an act of self-loathing performed to avoid punishment. But biblical repentance is not self-hatred; it is **return**.

The word itself means turning back.

This is why Scripture says:

"Return to me, and I will return to you," says Yahweh of Armies.
— **Book of Malachi 3:7 (WEB)**

God does not say, *"Prove yourself."*
He says, *"Come back."*

Repentance under restorative justice is not about earning forgiveness. It is about realignment with a God who is already inclined toward mercy.

Fear-based repentance produces shame.
Love-based repentance produces healing.

Trust Changes Everything

When fear is removed, faith changes shape.

- Prayer becomes conversation, not crisis management
- Obedience becomes response, not survival
- Scripture becomes guidance, not threat
- Community becomes support, not surveillance

Jesus describes this shift clearly:

"Come to me, all you who labor and are heavily burdened, and I will give you rest. Take my yoke upon you, and learn from me… and you will find rest for your souls."
— Gospel of Matthew 11:28–29 (WEB)

A yoke implies direction—but this yoke brings rest, not exhaustion. That alone should tell us something about the nature of God's authority.

Why Fear Persists

If fear-based faith is inconsistent with Scripture, why does it persist?

Because fear is an effective short-term motivator.
Because control is easier than trust.
Because systems benefit when people are afraid to question.

But fear cannot sustain genuine faith. It produces burnout, resentment, and eventually rejection.

Many people do not leave faith because they stop believing in God. They leave because they cannot reconcile fear-based religion with the God revealed in Jesus.

This book exists for those people.

Living as If God Is For You

Jeremiah records God's words to a fearful, displaced people:

"For I know the thoughts that I think toward you," says Yahweh,
"thoughts of peace, and not of evil,
to give you hope and a future."
— **Book of Jeremiah 29:11 (WEB)**

Living under this truth changes how a person moves through the world.

If God is for you:

- Failure is not fatal
- Growth is expected

- Questions are allowed
- Healing is possible
- The future is not closed

Faith becomes courage rooted in trust—not fear rooted in threat.

Re-centering the Heart of Faith

Faith without fear is not weak faith.
It is mature faith.

It does not deny accountability—it trusts God's character enough to face truth honestly. It does not avoid obedience—it understands obedience as alignment with love.

This is what it means to live under restorative justice.

Living Restored:? Justice, Mercy, and Human Continuity

Faith shaped by fear isolates people.
Faith shaped by love restores them.

When justice is understood as retribution, community becomes fragile. People protect themselves, keep score, hide weakness, and weaponize morality. Relationships turn transactional: approval is earned, failure is punished, and belonging is conditional.

But when justice is understood as restoration, community changes shape. Accountability remains—but it is exercised for healing, not humiliation. Truth is spoken—but it is aimed at reconciliation, not dominance.

This is not idealism. It is the natural outcome of living under the justice of a God who is slow to anger and rich in mercy.

The End of Scorekeeping

One of the clearest signs that justice has been misunderstood is **scorekeeping**—the quiet tallying of wrongs that fuels resentment, superiority, and exclusion.

Paul directly confronts this impulse:

"Love... takes no account of evil."
— **First Epistle to the Corinthians 13:5 (WEB)**

This does not mean wrongdoing is ignored. It means wrongdoing is not *stored* as ammunition.

Communities shaped by fear preserve records of failure to maintain control. Communities shaped by love address failure in order to restore trust.

God's justice does not keep score—so neither should communities that claim to reflect Him.

Forgiveness as a Communal Act

Forgiveness is often treated as a private spiritual exercise—something an individual does internally to find peace. Scripture presents forgiveness as something far more powerful and far more public.

Jesus teaches:

"For if you forgive men their trespasses, your heavenly Father will also forgive you. But if you don't forgive men their trespasses, neither will your Father forgive your trespasses."
— **Gospel of Matthew 6:14–15 (WEB)**

This is not a threat—it is a diagnosis.

Unforgiveness fractures community. It traps people in cycles of retaliation and distrust. A community that cannot forgive cannot heal.

Forgiveness is not denial of harm. It is the refusal to let harm dictate the future.

Accountability Without Shame

Fear-based systems rely on shame to enforce behavior. Shame says, *"You are the problem."* Restoration says, *"Something is broken—and it can be repaired."*

Scripture consistently rejects shame as a tool of justice.

Paul instructs communities to confront wrongdoing—but always with restoration as the goal:

"Brothers, even if a man is caught in some fault, you who are spiritual must restore such a one in a spirit of gentleness; looking to yourself, so that you also aren't tempted."
— Epistle to the Galatians 6:1 (WEB)

Notice the posture:

- Gentleness, not superiority
- Self-awareness, not condemnation
- Restoration, not expulsion

This mirrors God's own justice. Accountability exists—but it is exercised with humility and care.

Justice That Protects the Vulnerable

Restorative justice does not ignore harm—especially harm done to the vulnerable.

Scripture repeatedly insists that true justice defends those most easily exploited:

"Learn to do well. Seek justice. Relieve the oppressed. Judge the fatherless. Plead for the widow."
— **Book of Isaiah 1:17 (WEB)**

Justice rooted in love does not excuse abuse. It confronts it directly—because abuse destroys the very people God seeks to restore.

A community shaped by God's justice is not permissive; it is protective. It refuses to sacrifice the vulnerable to preserve comfort, reputation, or power.

Truth Without Violence

One of the great fears surrounding mercy is that it will undermine truth. But Scripture never asks communities to choose between honesty and compassion.

Jesus embodies both.

"The Word became flesh, and lived among us… full of grace and truth."
— **Gospel of John 1:14 (WEB)**

Grace without truth becomes sentimentality.
Truth without grace becomes brutality.

Restorative justice insists on both.

This means communities can:

- Name harm honestly
- Set boundaries clearly
- Protect those at risk
- And still seek redemption

This balance is difficult—but it is the way of Christ.

Bearing One Another's Burdens

Fear-based religion demands performance. Restorative faith makes room for weakness.

Paul instructs believers:

"Bear one another's burdens, and so fulfill the law of Christ."
— Epistle to the Galatians 6:2 (WEB)

The "law of Christ" is not control—it is love enacted through shared responsibility.

This is what community looks like when God is believed to be *for us*. People are not abandoned in failure. They are accompanied through it.

When Community Fails

It must be said plainly: Christian communities have often failed to live this vision. Fear, control, and exclusion have too often replaced patience, mercy, and restoration.

Scripture does not deny this possibility. It anticipates it.

Jesus warns against religious systems that "tie up heavy burdens" while refusing to help carry them. The Bible critiques its own communities relentlessly—not to destroy them, but to call them back.

Failure does not invalidate the vision. It reveals how urgently it is needed.

Community as Witness

A restored community is itself a testimony.

Jesus tells His followers:

"By this everyone will know that you are my disciples, if you have love for one another."
— **Gospel of John 13:35 (WEB)**

Not doctrinal precision.
Not moral superiority.
Not institutional strength.

Love.

When communities practice justice shaped by mercy, they demonstrate—without argument—that God is not against humanity.

Re-centering Our Shared Life

Living restored does not mean living without conflict. It means living with conflict guided by love rather than fear.

It means:

- Refusing to weaponize morality
- Rejecting shame as a tool
- Practicing forgiveness as strength
- Protecting the vulnerable fiercely
- Holding truth and grace together

This is justice as God intends it.

God Is For You

By now, one truth should be unmistakably clear: the Bible does not tell the story of an angry God barely tolerating humanity. It tells the story of a God who pursues, restores, and refuses to abandon the people He loves—even when that love is rejected.

From wisdom literature to prophecy, from Jesus' teaching to Paul's theology, from the cross to the resurrection, Scripture speaks with a consistent voice: **God's justice flows from His character, and His character is love—patient, merciful, slow to anger, and oriented toward restoration**.

This is not a selective reading. It is the Bible's own self-portrait.

Returning to the Beginning

Early in this book, we encountered a simple but profound statement:

"Many seek the ruler's favor,
but justice for man comes from Yahweh."
— **Book of Proverbs 29:26 (WEB)**

Everything we have explored flows from this truth.

Human power seeks compliance.
Divine justice seeks restoration.

Human authority often protects itself.
Divine authority gives itself away.

This distinction matters because so many people have walked away from faith—not because they rejected God, but because they were taught to fear Him.

Why the Bible Has Been Misread

The accusation that the Bible is outdated, harmful, or oppressive did not arise without reason. Scripture has been misused. God's name has been invoked to justify cruelty, silence questions, and enforce control.

But misuse does not define meaning.

A book designed to subjugate would not:

- Describe God as slow to anger repeatedly
- Critique corrupt leaders relentlessly
- Elevate mercy over sacrifice
- Present power as accountable
- Portray God grieving rejection rather than enforcing obedience
- Center salvation on self-giving love

The Bible contains its own safeguards against abuse. It exposes false authority. It condemns exploitation. It insists that justice belongs to God—not to those who claim His name.

The Cross Revisited—One Last Time

If there is any doubt about God's posture toward humanity, the cross resolves it.

At the cross:

- God does not retaliate
- God does not coerce
- God does not dominate
- God absorbs injustice
- God forgives enemies
- God restores relationship

"God demonstrates his own love toward us, in that while we were yet sinners, Christ died for us."
— **Epistle to the Romans 5:8 (WEB)**

A God who sacrifices Himself rather than destroy His enemies is not against humanity.

He is for it—at immeasurable cost.

The Resurrection's Final Word

The resurrection confirms that love was not naïve and mercy was not misplaced.

God does not erase justice—He fulfills it.
God does not ignore evil—He overcomes it.
God does not abandon humanity—He redeems it.

"He is not here, but has risen."
— **Gospel of Luke 24:6 (WEB)**

This is God's final verdict on humanity: **life, not death**.

What This Means for You

If God is for you, then fear no longer gets the final word.

- Failure is not fatal
- Doubt is not disqualifying
- Questions are not betrayal
- Growth is expected
- Healing is possible

Faith becomes trust, not terror.
Obedience becomes alignment, not submission.
Justice becomes healing, not revenge.

This does not mean life is easy. It means you are not alone—and you are not the enemy.

God's Intention Has Always Been Clear

Through the prophet Jeremiah, God speaks to a people who are afraid, displaced, and uncertain about the future:

"For I know the thoughts that I think toward you," says Yahweh,
"thoughts of peace, and not of evil,
to give you hope and a future."
— **Book of Jeremiah 29:11 (WEB)**

These words are not sentimental. They are covenantal. They reveal intent.

God's intention toward humanity has never been destruction. It has always been restoration.

A Faith Worth Trusting

If Christianity were built on fear, it would collapse under honest scrutiny.
If the Bible were built on lies, the cross would be meaningless.
If God were cruel, love would be a contradiction.

But the story Scripture tells—when read as a whole—is coherent, consistent, and compelling.

It is the story of a God who:

- Creates freely
- Judges justly
- Loves patiently
- Forgives radically

- Restores completely

This is not a God to be feared into obedience.
This is a God to be trusted into transformation.

An Invitation, Not a Threat

The Bible does not end with a command to be afraid.
It ends with an invitation.

"The Spirit and the bride say, 'Come!' He who hears, let him say, 'Come!' He who is thirsty, let him come."
— **Book of Revelation 22:17 (WEB)**

God does not force Himself on anyone.
He invites.

He always has.

The Final Word

This book was written to say one thing clearly, gently, and honestly:

God is not against you.
He never has been.

Justice comes from Him because love comes from Him.
And love—true love—is always for life.

If you have been afraid of God, you have not seen Him clearly.
If you have been hurt in His name, He grieves that

harm.

If you are tired, uncertain, or searching—He is not standing in your way.

He is calling you home.

What You Thought Was Against You Was Guarding You

Understanding rarely comes all at once. More often, it arrives quietly—after resistance softens, after fear loosens its grip, after pieces that once seemed contradictory begin to align. This book has not asked you to suspend reason or silence doubt. It has asked you to look again—carefully, honestly, and without the assumptions that so often distort what Scripture is actually saying.

And when everything is finally placed side by side—God's character, God's justice, Jesus' teaching, the cross, the resurrection, love, mercy, patience—something becomes clear:

The Bible was never written to harm you.
It was written to protect you.

The Root of the Misunderstanding

Many people do not reject God because they are immoral, rebellious, or unwilling to submit. They reject God because they believe the Bible presents Him as unpredictable, angry, and dangerous—someone whose rules exist to limit freedom rather than preserve life.

That belief does not come from nowhere. It grows wherever Scripture is reduced to control, wherever fear replaces trust, wherever authority is mistaken for holiness. Over time, guidance begins to feel like threat. Correction begins to feel like condemnation. Protection begins to feel like restriction.

When that happens, the Bible stops sounding like good news.

But what if the problem was never the text—only the lens through which it was read?

A Guide Is Only Oppressive If You Don't Trust Its Intent

Every boundary communicates intent.

A guardrail on a mountain road can feel restrictive—until you understand what it's guarding against. A warning label can feel limiting—until you understand the damage it prevents. A map can feel confining—until you realize it keeps you from getting lost.

The Bible functions this way.

It does not exist to narrow human life, but to **preserve it**. Its commands are not traps; they are guardrails. Its warnings are not threats; they are acts of care. Its moral vision is not arbitrary; it is calibrated to human flourishing.

"Yahweh's law is perfect, restoring the soul.
Yahweh's covenant is sure, making wise the simple."
— **Book of Psalms 19:7 (WEB)**

Restoration—not restriction—is the goal.

Justice Was Never About God Turning on You

One of the greatest distortions of Scripture is the belief that God's justice exists primarily to punish humanity. That justice is something to fear because it is directed *at* us.

But throughout this book, a different picture has emerged.

Justice in the Bible exists because God is **for humanity**, not against it. Justice opposes whatever deforms human life—violence, deceit, exploitation, pride, cruelty—not because God is angry at people, but because He values them.

God's justice is not aimed at destroying you.
It is aimed at destroying what destroys you.

"Yahweh is gracious and merciful,
slow to anger, and abundant in loving kindness."
— **Book of Psalms 145:8 (WEB)**

A God slow to anger is not lying in wait for failure. He is restraining judgment to make room for restoration.

Jesus Did Not Change God—He Revealed Him

Some assume the Old Testament presents a harsh God, while Jesus introduces a gentler one. But this book has shown something else entirely: **Jesus reveals what God has always been like**.

The patience, mercy, restraint, and compassion seen in Christ are not new attributes. They are ancient ones—woven through the Law, the Prophets, and the Psalms.

Jesus does not correct God's temperament.
He **clarifies it**.

"He who has seen me has seen the Father."
— **Gospel of John 14:9 (WEB)**

If Jesus gathers rather than coerces, forgives rather than retaliates, and absorbs injustice rather than returns it, then this is who God has always been.

The Cross Was Not God Losing Control

For many, the cross is the most troubling symbol in Christianity. It looks like violence sanctified. Like suffering demanded. Like love compromised.

But when seen through the lens of restorative justice, the cross changes meaning entirely.

The cross is not God lashing out.
It is God stepping in.

It is not punishment inflicted on an unwilling victim. It is love willingly entering human violence to end its power.

"God was in Christ, reconciling the world to himself."
— Second Epistle to the Corinthians 5:19 (WEB)

A God who enters suffering to heal it is not against humanity. He is profoundly, irrevocably **for it**.

Resurrection Reveals God's Endgame

If the cross shows God's willingness to suffer with humanity, the resurrection shows God's refusal to abandon it.

The resurrection is not a miracle added to make Christianity more hopeful. It is the **logical outcome** of a God committed to restoration.

It declares that:

- Death does not define us
- Failure is not final
- Injustice does not win
- Love is stronger than fear

God's final word is not condemnation.

"He is not here, but has risen."
— Gospel of Luke 24:6 (WEB)

This is what it means for God to be for you.

Why the Bible Sometimes Feels Uncomfortable

A protective guide will often confront us.

The Bible challenges pride.
It exposes self-deception.
It disrupts destructive habits.
It calls out injustice—even when we benefit from it.

That discomfort is not harm.
It is **intervention**.

Just as a physician may cause pain to heal, Scripture sometimes presses where it hurts—not to wound, but to restore.

"Faithful are the wounds of a friend."
— **Book of Proverbs 27:6 (WEB)**

The Bible does not comfort us by affirming every desire. It comforts us by **leading us toward life**.

What Changes When You Finally See It

When you realize the Bible is a guide and not a threat, everything shifts.

- God becomes understandable, not terrifying
- Faith becomes trust, not anxiety
- Obedience becomes alignment, not submission

- Repentance becomes return, not humiliation
- Justice becomes healing, not revenge

Suddenly, Scripture reads less like a list of prohibitions and more like a path home.

"Your word is a lamp to my feet,
and a light for my path."
— **Book of Psalms 119:105 (WEB)**

Light exists to guide, not to blind.

The "Ah" Moment

The moment of clarity—the *"Ah, I get it now"*—comes when you see that what once felt threatening was actually **protective**, and what once felt oppressive was actually **restorative**.

God was never trying to corner you.
He was trying to keep you from falling.
He was never trying to dominate you.
He was trying to guard what was precious.

You.

A Final Reframing

The Bible is not a weapon pointed at humanity.
It is a map offered to it.

God is not standing over you in judgment.
He is walking with you in love.

"Yahweh is good to all.
His tender mercies are over all his works."
— **Book of Psalms 145:9 (WEB)**

That includes you.

The Last Thing to Remember

If you take nothing else from this book, take this:

**God's justice exists because His love exists.
And His love exists because He is for you.**

Not to harm you.
Not to control you.
Not to confuse you.

But to lead you—patiently, faithfully, and gently—back into life.

And now, perhaps for the first time, you can see it clearly.

Made in the USA
Coppell, TX
19 February 2026

71799129R00059